Energy in the Factory

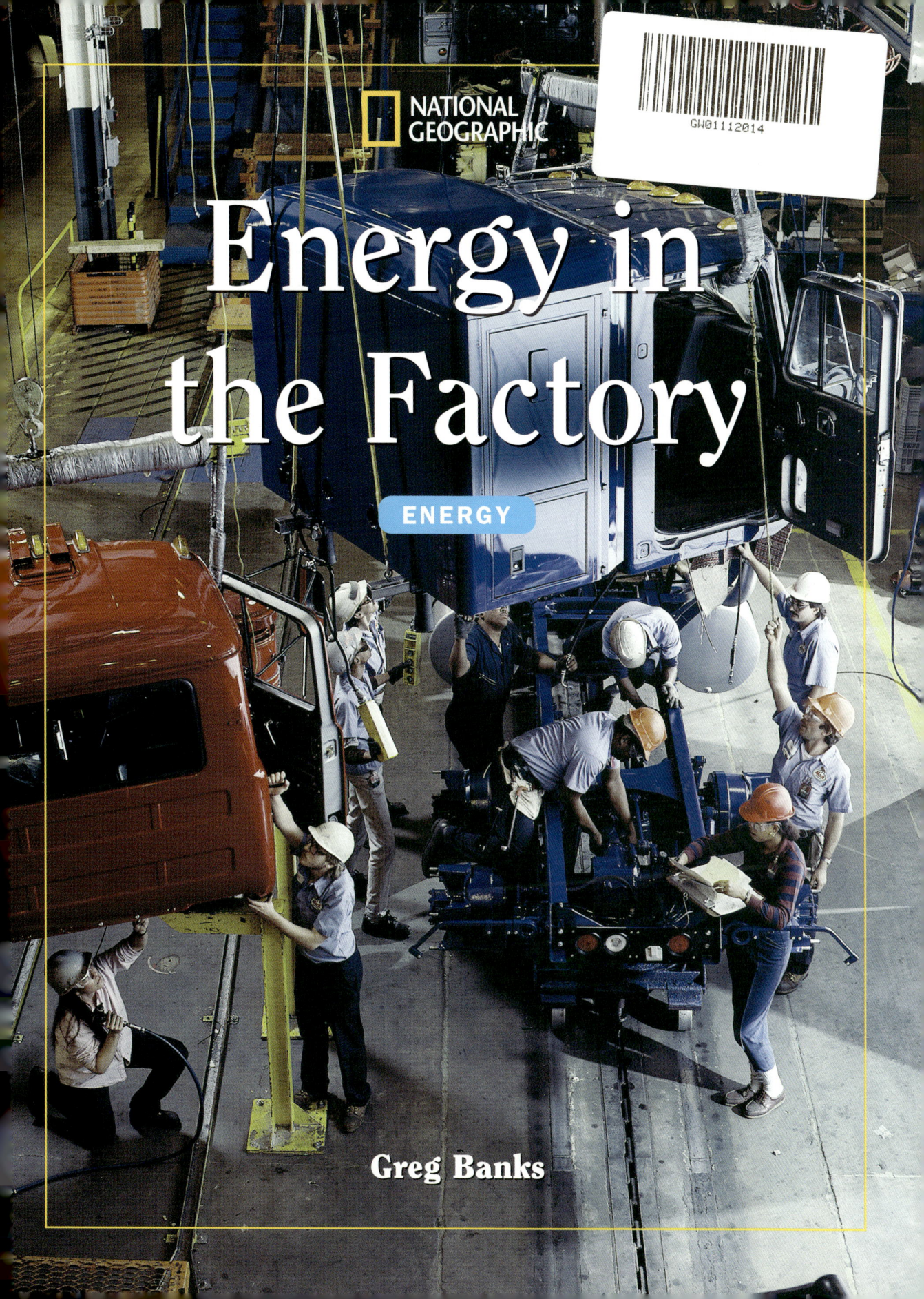

ENERGY

Greg Banks

PICTURE CREDITS
Cover: woman processing packages at warehouse distribution center © Roger Tully/Stone/Getty Images.

page 1 © William Taufic/Corbis/Tranz; page 4 (bottom left) © Michael Pohuski/FoodPix/Getty Images; page 4 (bottom right), Digital Vision; page 5 (top), Digital Vision; page 5 (bottom left), PhotoAlto; page 5 (bottom right), Photodisc; page 6, Digital Vision; page 7 (top left), Digital Vision; page 7 (top middle), Corbis; page 7 (top right), Brand X Pictures; page 7 (bottom left), Lester Lefkowitz/Corbis/Tranz; page 7 (bottom right), Photodisc; page 8 © Annie Griffiths Belt/Corbis/Tranz; page 9, Digital Vision; page 10 © Charles O'Rear/Corbis/Tranz; page 11 © John Henley/Corbis/Tranz; page 14 © Cameron/Corbis/Tranz; page 15, Photodisc; page 16, Priddy Bicknell; page 19 (top), Digital Vision; page 19 (bottom left), Corbis; page 19 (bottom right), Photodisc; page 21 © Chris McCooey/Stone/Getty Images; page 22 © Lester Lefkowitz/Corbis/Tranz; page 23 © Stephen Simpson/Taxi/Getty Images; page 24 © T.C. Malhotra/Getty Images; page 25 © David McNew/Newsmakers/Getty Images; page 26 © Charles Rotkin/Corbis/Tranz; page 29 © Charles Gupton/Corbis/Tranz.

Produced through the worldwide resources of the National Geographic Society, John M. Fahey, Jr., President and Chief Executive Officer; Gilbert M. Grosvenor, Chairman of the Board.

PREPARED BY NATIONAL GEOGRAPHIC SCHOOL PUBLISHING
Sheron Long, Chief Executive Officer; Samuel Gesumaria, President; Steve Mico, Executive Vice President and Publisher; Francis Downey, Editor in Chief; Richard Easby, Editorial Manager; Margaret Sidlosky, Director of Design and Illustrations; Jim Hiscott, Design Manager; Cynthia Olson and Ruth Ann Thompson, Art Directors; Matt Wascavage, Director of Publishing Services; Lisa Pergolizzi, Production Manager.

MANUFACTURING AND QUALITY CONTROL
Christopher A. Liedel, Chief Financial Officer; Phillip L. Schlosser, Vice President; Clifton M. Brown III, Director.

EDITOR
Mary Anne Wengel

PROGRAMME CONSULTANTS
Dr. Shirley V. Dickson, National Literacy Consultant; James A. Shymansky, E. Desmond Lee Professor of Science Education, University of Missouri-St Louis.

Copyright © 2007 Macmillan Education Australia.

First published in 2007 in Great Britain by Kingscourt/McGraw-Hill publishers.

McGraw-Hill International (UK) Limited
McGraw-Hill House
Shoppenhangers Road, Maidenhead
Berkshire, SL6 2QL

www.kingscourt.co.uk

The materials in this publication may be photocopied for use only within the purchasing organisation. Otherwise, all rights reserved and no part of the publication may be reproduced, stored in a retrieval system or transmitted, in any form, or by any means, electronic, mechanical, photocopying, recording or otherwise, without prior permission of the publishers. National Geographic, National Geographic Explorer, and the Yellow Border are trademarks of the National Geographic Society.

ISBN–13: 978-1-4202-1846-6

Printed in Hong Kong.

2011 2010 2009 2008 2007
1 2 3 4 5 6 7 8 9 10 11 12 13 14 15

Contents

- Energy 4
- Energy in the Factory 6
- Think About the Key Concepts 17

Visual Literacy
Photograph Montage 18

Genre Study
Pro-Con Articles 20

Water Energy 21

- Apply the Key Concepts 27

Research and Write
Write Your Own Pro-Con Article 28

Glossary 31

Index 32

Energy

Think of all the things that move. People move their bodies. Cars drive along the road. Rain falls to the ground. But do you know what is involved in all this movement? The answer is energy. Energy is involved in everything that happens. Energy is all around you. You will find energy in your home, in factories, at airports, and in sports arenas.

Key Concepts

1. Energy is the ability to do work.
2. There are different forms and sources of energy.
3. Energy can change from one form to another.

Where Energy Is Found

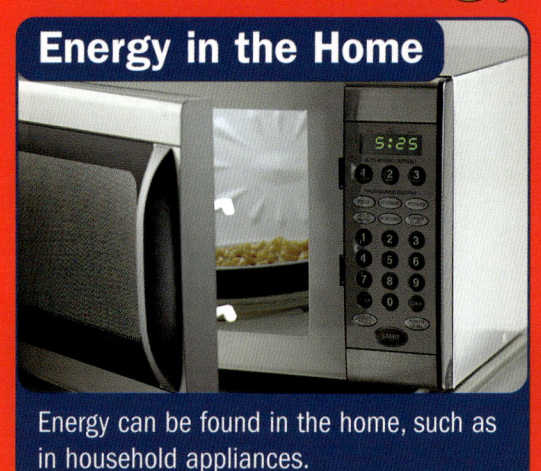

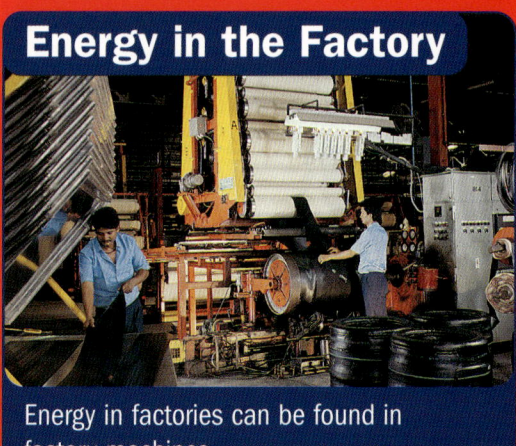

Energy in the Home

Energy can be found in the home, such as in household appliances.

Energy in the Factory

Energy in factories can be found in factory machines.

In this book you will learn about sources and users of energy in the factory, such as this welding machine.

Energy at the Airport

Energy at airports exists in computers and airplanes.

Energy at the Sports Arena

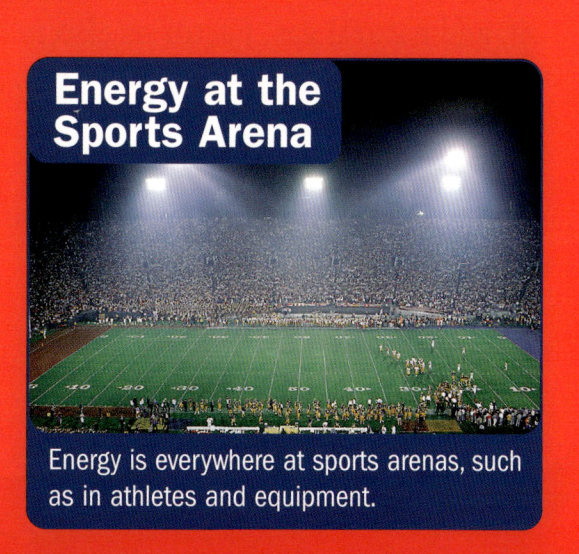

Energy is everywhere at sports arenas, such as in athletes and equipment.

Energy in the Factory

Think about a factory. Factories are places where people make goods. Many machines are used in factories. In some factories, large furnaces are used to melt metals and glass. In others, conveyer belts carry goods from one place to another. Factories use many different machines to do many different tasks. But all these machines have one thing in common. They all use energy. Without energy, none of these machines would run.

Many factory machines get the energy they need from electricity. Other machines, like furnaces, get energy by burning **fuels**. These fuels include coal, oil, and natural gas. Factories also need a lot of light. Light fixtures need energy so that they can provide light. Without energy, the machines in factories would not be able to run.

Factory lights use energy.

Here are some pictures of items in and around factories that use energy. What others can you name?

Energy Users in the Factory

Crane

Furnace

Tools

Conveyor belt

Forklift

Key Concept 1 Energy is the ability to do work.

Energy, Force, and Work

Energy, **force**, and **work** have special meanings in science. In science, energy is the ability to do work. Do you know how energy and work are related? To understand the connection, you first need to understand about force.

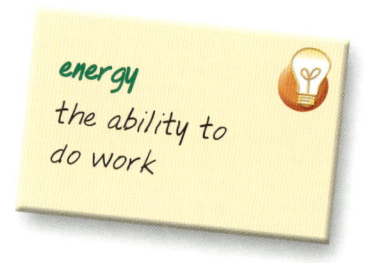

> **energy**
> the ability to do work

In science, force is something that makes an object move, stop, or change. When you hammer a nail into wood, you are using force. When you stop a door from closing, you are using force. When you lift an object from the floor, you are also using force.

> **work**
> what results when force moves, stops, or changes an object

These men use force to lift a pallet.

When a person or a machine uses force to make something move, stop, or change, work is being done. If nothing is moved, stopped, or changed, then no work is done. Whenever work is done, though, we know that energy is involved. We also know that it takes more energy to do more work. So people and machines use energy to do work. A person uses energy to tighten a screw. A forklift uses energy to start, move, stop, and lift things.

Forklifts use energy to lift and move objects.

Key Concept 2 There are different forms and sources of energy.

Basic Forms of Energy

There are two basic forms of energy. One form depends on the motion of things. The other depends on the position of things.

Kinetic Energy

The first type of energy is called **kinetic energy**. Kinetic energy is the energy of motion. All moving objects have kinetic energy. Everything that moves in a factory also has kinetic energy. The machines and the people who use them have kinetic energy when they move. A robot building cars in a car factory has kinetic energy when its parts move.

The amount of kinetic energy a moving object has depends on two things. One thing is how big the object is. The other thing is how fast the object moves. The bigger an object is and the faster it moves, the more kinetic energy it has.

Robots have many moving parts. They have kinetic energy as they assemble a car.

Potential Energy

The other basic type of energy is called **potential energy**. Potential energy is energy that is stored. When potential energy is released, or let out, it can do work. Imagine a huge hammer used to flatten out metal in a factory. The hammer is given potential energy when it is lifted above the metal. The higher the hammer is lifted, the more potential, or stored, energy it has.

As the hammer begins to move down, its energy changes. It changes from stored potential energy to kinetic energy of motion.

A raised hammer has potential energy.

Some Sources of Energy

Energy can be stored and released in different ways.

Chemical Energy

Fuels, such as coal and oil, are used to heat furnaces in factories. Coal and oil are examples of stored, or potential, chemical energy. Chemicals in coal or oil react, or change, when they are burned. This chemical reaction causes energy to be released. This energy is released as heat and light. The heat is used to melt metals in furnaces.

Electrical Energy

Think of all the machines, lights, and computers that are used in a factory. Most of these use electrical energy to work. Electricity involves the flow of **electrons**. An electron is one of the particles that make up an **atom**. This flow of electrons releases energy. Electrical energy travels to factories along power lines.

Movement of Electrical Energy

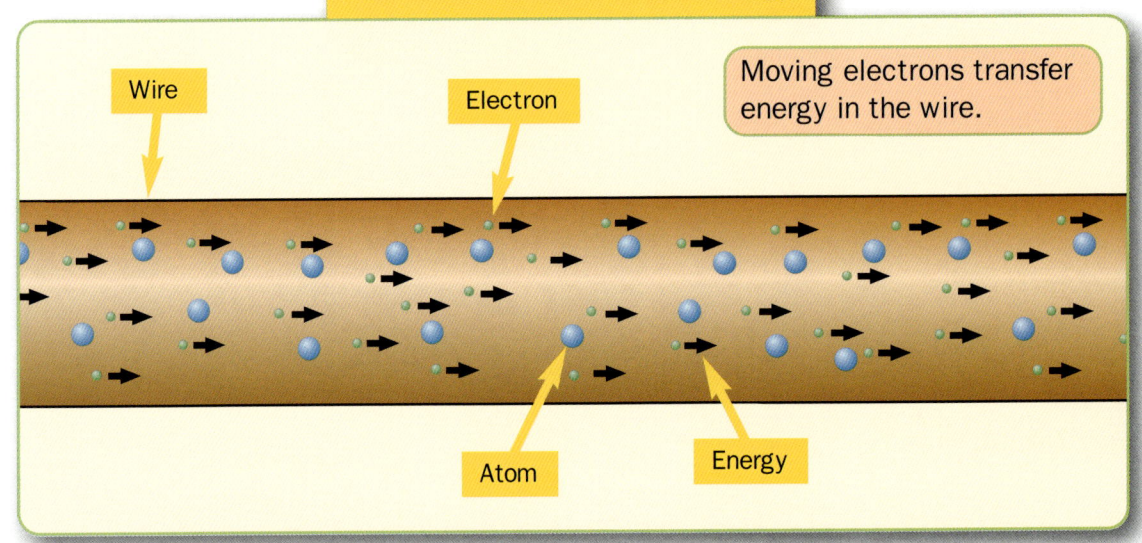

Wire

Electron

Moving electrons transfer energy in the wire.

Atom

Energy

Heat Flow in Matter

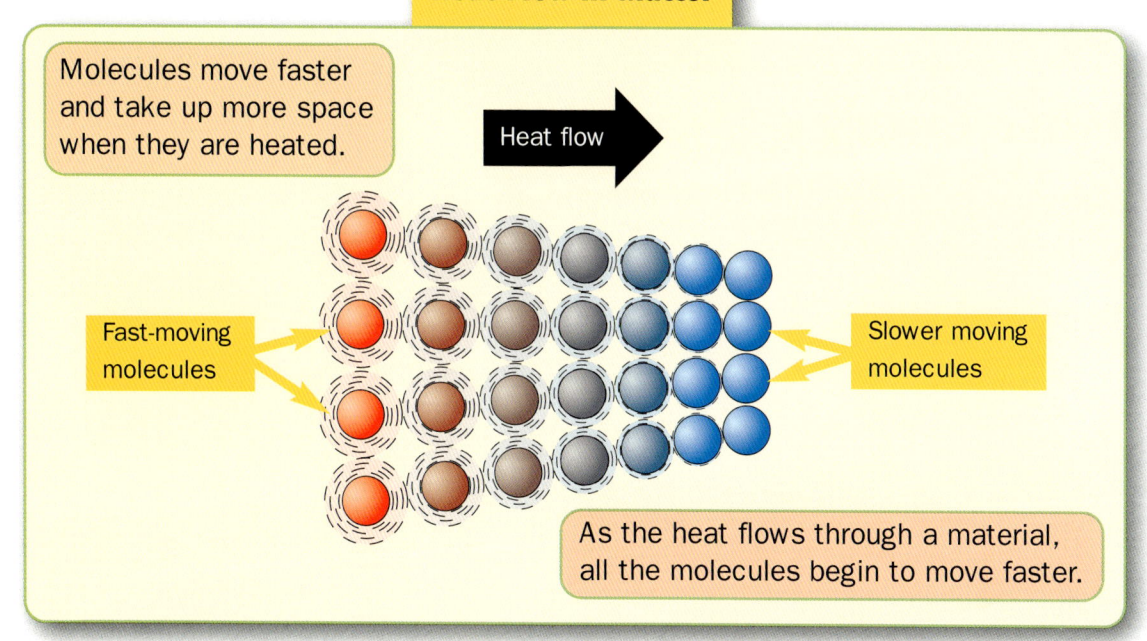

Molecules move faster and take up more space when they are heated.

Heat flow →

Fast-moving molecules

Slower moving molecules

As the heat flows through a material, all the molecules begin to move faster.

Heat Energy

Heat energy is often used in factories to make things. All objects are made up of clusters of particles called **molecules**. If heat is added to the object, the molecules will begin to move faster. The temperature then rises as the molecules move faster. The increased warmth is heat energy.

Heat energy always moves from hotter places to cooler places. In factories, solid materials are melted or shaped by adding heat energy from fuels.

Light Energy

There is one form of energy you can see. It is called light energy. Light energy travels in waves from a light source. The sun is the source of most light. One type of light energy used in factories is **lasers**. Lasers are very intense light beams. They can do work like cutting through metals.

Key Concept 3 Energy can change from one form to another.

How Energy Changes

Energy does not always stay in one form. Energy can change from one form to another. Energy changes when the lights are switched on in a factory. The electrical energy causes a **filament**, or wire, in a lightbulb to heat up. The heat energy causes the filament to glow. The glowing filament gives off light energy. So the electrical energy has changed first to heat energy and then to light energy.

In a lightbulb, electrical energy changes to heat energy and then to light energy.

Sometimes one form of energy can change into many forms of energy. In factories, people use electric drills to drill holes. Electrical energy changes to kinetic energy when the drill bit moves to cut the hole. Some of the electrical energy becomes sound energy. This is the noise the drill makes. After the drill has been used, it will feel warm. This warmth is heat energy. So the electrical energy has also changed to heat energy.

Electric drills use energy that changes form.

Less Useful Energy Changes

When energy changes from one form to another, the process is never 100 percent **efficient**. In other words, not all the energy that is changed is useful. As a result, when energy changes form, there is less energy to do work.

Think of a forklift in a factory that is powered by a gasoline engine. The chemical energy in the gasoline changes to kinetic energy as the forklift moves and does work. But not all the chemical energy changes into kinetic energy. Some of the chemical energy changes into heat energy. The engine becomes hot to the touch. But this heat energy is not useful. It does not help the machine do work.

Some of the chemical energy of gasoline in forklifts changes to wasted heat energy.

Think About the Key Concepts

Think about what you read. Think about the pictures and diagrams. Use these to answer the questions. Share what you think with others.

1. What is force? How is force related to energy and work?

2. Tell how the two basic forms of energy are different from each other.

3. Name two sources of energy and give an example of how each one works.

4. What are some examples of energy changing form?

VISUAL LITERACY

Photograph Montage

A photograph montage is a collection of photographs. The photographs show different things related to the same topic. The caption tells you what each photograph shows.

The photograph montage on page 19 shows different sources of energy that are found or used in the factory. Look back at the photograph montage on page 7. It shows different objects found in the factory that use energy.

How to Read a Photograph Montage

1. **Read the title.**
   The title tells you the topic of the photograph montage.
2. **Read the caption.**
   The caption tells you what each photograph shows.
3. **Think about what you have learned.**
   Think about how the different photographs are related to each other. Think of any other photographs that could fit well into the photograph montage.

Sources of Energy in the Factory

1
2
3
4

1. Furnace – heat energy; 2. Computers – light and sound energy; 3. Coal – chemical energy; 4. Lasers – light energy

Study the Montage

Study the photograph montage by following the steps on page 18. Write down the different sources of energy that are found in the factory. Write down another example of each source of energy in the factory. Share your ideas with a classmate.

GENRE STUDY

Pro-Con Articles

A pro-con article gives information on both sides of a problem or issue. The "pro" side has arguments in favor of the issue. The "con" side has arguments against the issue. The article does not try to persuade readers about the issue. Readers must make up their own minds after reading through all the arguments.

A pro-con article usually contains the following elements:

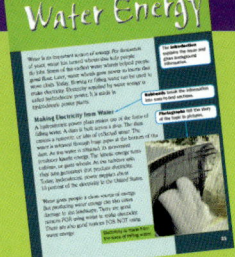

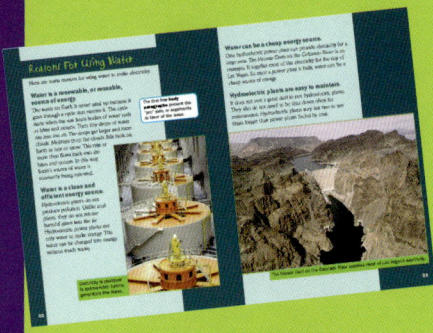

Introduction
The introduction explains the issue and gives background information to help readers understand it. The introduction may be three or four paragraphs long.

Body Paragraphs
The first few body paragraphs present the "pro" arguments. The next few body paragraphs present the "con" arguments.

The Conclusion
The conclusion briefly summarizes both sides of the issue.

Water Energy

Water is an important source of energy. For thousands of years, water has turned wheels that help people do jobs. Some of the earliest waterwheels helped people grind flour. Later, waterwheels gave power to looms that wove cloth. Today, flowing or falling water can be used to make electricity. Electricity supplied by water energy is called hydroelectric power. It is made in hydroelectric power plants.

The **introduction** explains the issue and gives background information.

Making Electricity from Water

A hydroelectric power plant makes use of the force of falling water. A dam is built across a river. The dam creates a reservoir, or lake of collected water. The water is released through huge pipes at the bottom of the dam. As the water is released, its movement produces kinetic energy. The kinetic energy turns turbines, or giant wheels. As the turbines spin, they turn generators that produce electricity. Today, hydroelectric power supplies about 10 percent of the electricity in the United States.

Water gives people a clean source of energy. But producing water energy can also cause damage to the landscape. There are good reasons FOR using water to make electricity. There are also good reasons FOR NOT using water energy.

Subheads break the information into easy-to-find sections.

Photographs tell the story of the topic in pictures.

Electricity is made from the force of falling water.

Reasons For Using Water

Here are some reasons for using water to make electricity.

Water is a renewable, or reusable, source of energy.

The water on Earth is never used up because it goes through a cycle that renews it. The cycle starts when the sun heats bodies of water such as lakes and oceans. Then tiny drops of water rise into the air. The drops get larger and form clouds. Moisture from the clouds falls back on Earth as rain or snow. This rain or snow then flows back into the lakes and oceans. In this way, Earth's source of water is constantly being renewed.

> The first few **body paragraphs** present the "pro" side, or arguments in favor of the issue.

Water is a clean and efficient energy source.

Hydroelectric plants do not produce pollution. Unlike coal plants, they do not release harmful gases into the air. Hydroelectric power plants use only water to make energy. This water can be changed into energy without much waste.

Electricity is produced in hydroelectric turbine generators like these.

Water can be a cheap energy source.

One hydroelectric power plant can provide electricity for a large area. The Hoover Dam on the Colorado River is an example. It supplies most of the electricity for the city of Las Vegas. So once a power plant is built, water can be a cheap source of energy.

Hydroelectric plants are easy to maintain.

It does not cost a great deal to run hydroelectric plants. They also do not need to be shut down often for maintenance. Hydroelectric plants may last two to ten times longer than power plants fueled by coal.

The Hoover Dam on the Colorado River supplies most of Las Vegas's electricity.

Reasons For Not Using Water

Here are some reasons for not using water to make electricity.

Hydroelectric power plants drive animals and people out of an area.

When hydroelectric power plants are built, reservoirs are created to store water. To create the reservoirs, some areas of land are flooded. As a result, the habitats, or homes, of many animals are lost. For example, fish populations can be harmed if fish cannot get past the dam.

People living in the area where the reservoir is created have to move to other places. They lose their homes and often their jobs. Sometimes local cultures and historical sites also get destroyed. Recreational activities, such as fishing and swimming in the river, may also be threatened.

> The next few **body paragraphs** present the "con" side, or arguments against the issue.

These people are protesting against dams being built on the Narmada River in India.

Hydroelectric power plants break up the flow of water to other areas.

When a river is dammed, large amounts of water go into the reservoir. This lessens the flow of water to other areas that may need or want it. The area below the dam may get much less water than before. Plants and animals may live there, but life becomes harder because there is less water. Land once used for farming may become less fertile and even dry out.

Hydroelectric plants can only be built in places where there is enough water.

Hydroelectric plants work only in areas with a large supply of water from rivers. The area must also receive plenty of rainfall. If there is drought, or a serious rain shortage, there may not be enough water to produce electricity.

Hydroelectric plants take up a great deal of space.

Most hydroelectric plants are huge structures. If an area is already crowded with houses, a large hydroelectric plant cannot be built there. When plants are constructed, they are often visible for miles around. So the entire landscape of an area can change.

Droughts cause rivers to dry up. Without rain, hydroelectric plants struggle to produce electricity.

RESEARCH AND WRITE

Write Your Own Pro-Con Article

You have read about the pros and cons of using water to make electricity. Now, you can research another use of natural resources to get energy. Get ready to write your own pro-con article.

1. Study the Model

Look back at pages 21–26. Study the organization of the article. Notice how the introduction explains how water is used to make electricity. Now look at the first several body paragraphs. They present reasons for using water. The next several body paragraphs give reasons not to use water. The paper ends with a conclusion that summarizes both points of view. You will want to follow this organization in your own pro-con article.

Writing a Pro-Con Article

- Write two or three introductory paragraphs that give background information.
- Write several "pro" paragraphs that give arguments in favor of the issue.
- Next, write several "con" paragraphs that give arguments against the issue.
- Summarize both sides of the issue in your conclusion.

2. Choose Your Topic

Think about all the different resources people can use to make electricity. They may use coal energy, nuclear energy, or solar energy. Choose one of these ways to make electricity that you are interested in. Your article will be about the pros and cons of using this resource to make electricity.

3. Research Your Topic

Start by getting background information about your resource. Use the library or the Internet. Find out how long the resource has been used and how many people get electricity from it. Next, look for pro and con information about the resource. Find three or four things that make it a good source of electricity. Then find three or four reasons not to use it. Look for information about cost, how much of the resource is available, and issues with the environment. Organize your points in a chart.

Using Coal Energy	
Pros	Cons
• plentiful supply	• damages the environment

4. Write a Draft

Look over the information you have found. Put the important background facts into your introduction. Then write the pro and con arguments. Present the same number of pro points as con points. Finally, write a conclusion that summarizes both sides of the argument.

5. Revise and Edit

Read your draft. Does it give good background information? Make sure it shows each side of the issue fairly. Correct any mistakes in your spelling or punctuation.

SHARING YOUR WORK

Hold an Energy Debate

A debate is a meeting where two people or groups each present and defend a different side of an argument. Now that you have written about a type of energy, you can get together with other students who wrote on the same topic and have an energy debate.

How to Hold a Debate

1. **Form topic groups.**
   Form groups according to the writing topic. Then divide these groups into two: those students who will discuss the pro side and those who will discuss the con side.

2. **Organize your information.**
   Work in these small groups to develop a pro or con argument on your energy topic. Make a list of all the pros or cons each member of the group thought of.

3. **Plan your argument.**
   As a group, decide which pros or cons would make the strongest argument. Organize these issues into a presentation.

4. **Get ready to present your pro or con argument.**
   Choose a person from the group to be the speaker. This person can practice reading the argument while other group members give feedback. Those who are not presenting should prepare to answer questions from the class.

5. **Present your pro or con arguments.**
   The two speakers from either side of the issue will present their arguments to the class. The rest of the class can ask questions of the other group members once both sides of the argument have been presented. Then the class can vote on which side gave the strongest argument on the issue.

Glossary

atom – the tiniest unit of matter

efficient – being effective with little energy or time wasted

electrons – the smallest parts that make up an atom

energy – the ability to do work

filament – the thin wire inside a lightbulb that gives off light energy when heated

force – something that causes, changes, or stops the movement of an object

fuels – materials that are used as sources of energy

kinetic energy – the energy of motion

lasers – objects that make very narrow beams of strong light

molecules – small parts of matter, made up of two or more atoms

potential energy – stored energy

work – what results when force moves, stops, or changes an object

Index

chemical energy 12, 16

electrical energy 12, 14–15

forklift 7, 9, 16

fuels 6, 12–13

furnace 6–7, 12

heat energy 13–16

kinetic energy 10–11, 15–16

light energy 13–14

molecules 13

potential energy 11–12